HOW DO CELL PHONES WORK?

Technology Book for Kids
Children's How Things Work Books

BABY PROFESSOR
EDUCATION KIDS

Speedy Publishing LLC

40 E. Main St. #1156

Newark, DE 19711

www.speedypublishing.com

Copyright 2018

In this book, we're going to talk about how cell phones work. So, let's get right to it!

Cell phones have dramatically altered the way people live and work. Now it's possible to stay in touch with anyone in the world, no matter where you are, as long as you can get a signal on your cell phone. At the current time, it's estimated that over 5 billion people around the world own cell phones.

In fact, in developing countries over 90 percent of the phones used are cell phones, since these countries don't have the infrastructure of large networks of landlines.

Landlines are the types of lines you need to use telephones that are wired to the wall. Cell phones are also called cellular phones or mobile phones. Today, most of the cell phones used around the world are also smart phones.

HOW DO CELL PHONES WORK?

Cell phones are actually telephones that work by radio. Their calls are routed through a network connected to a main network of public telephones. Phones that are attached to landlines work in a very different way than cell phones work.

Imagine that you are sitting at a desk in an office. There is a telephone at the desk and it is attached to a landline. These landlines carry your phone calls using cables that are electrical.

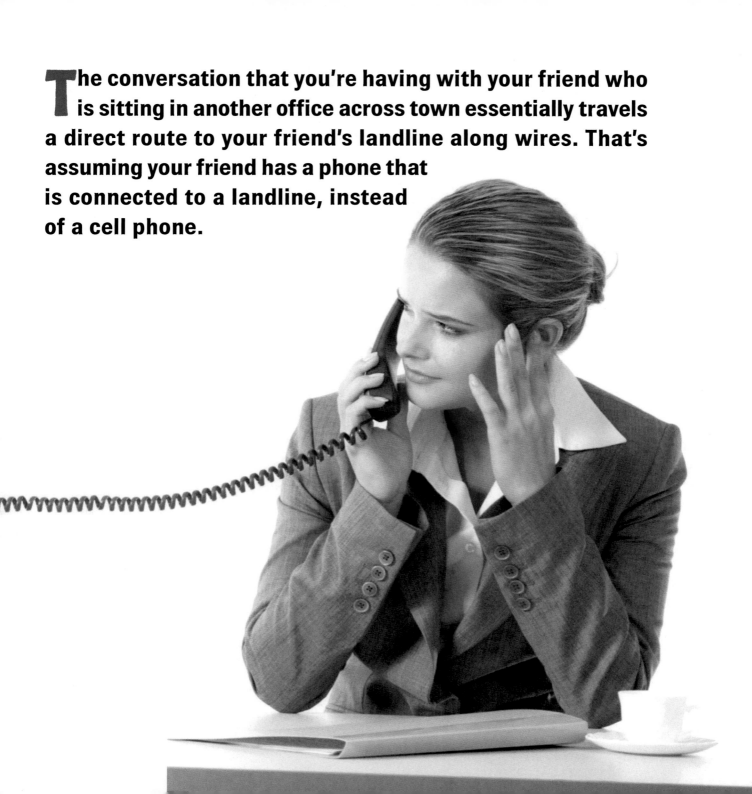

The conversation that you're having with your friend who is sitting in another office across town essentially travels a direct route to your friend's landline along wires. That's assuming your friend has a phone that is connected to a landline, instead of a cell phone.

Of course, this is a simplification since there are satellites as well as fiber-optic cables and other ways that these landlines connect throughout the network, but essentially your voice goes through your

FIBER OPTIC CABLES

phone from one landline to another to have a back-and-forth conversation with your friend on his or her landline phone.

A cell phone doesn't need any wires to operate. It uses radio waves, which are electromagnetic, to transmit and receive sounds. Energy from electromagnetic waves is everywhere around us. You can't see these waves, but they're surrounding you when you're sitting at home watching television, walking to school, or traveling on a train.

Lots of objects in our surroundings work using electromagnetic waves. Television broadcasts, radio programs, wireless doorbells, and toys controlled by radio all work through processes that use electromagnetic energy.

MASTER CONTROL IN A TELEVISION STUDIO

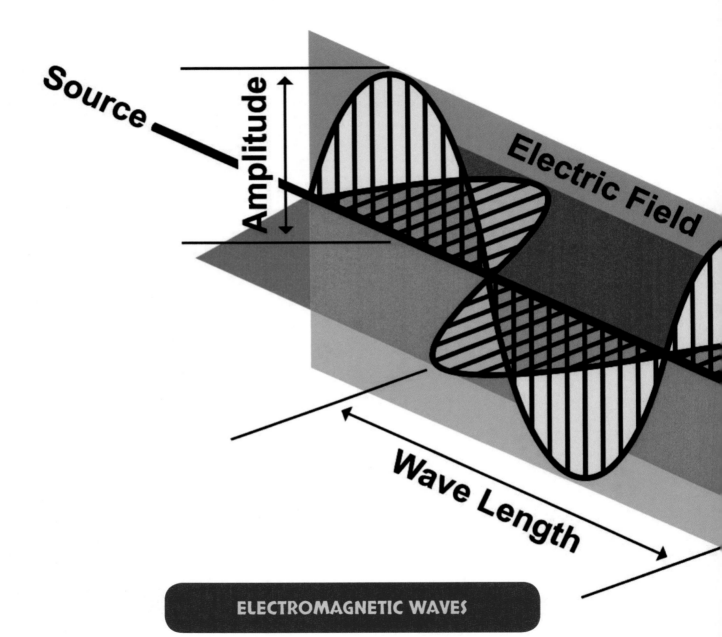

Source

Amplitude

Electric Field

Wave Length

ELECTROMAGNETIC WAVES

These invisible waves travel across space at light's speed, which is 186,000 miles every second. Cell phones use this energy to send your voice from one location to another.

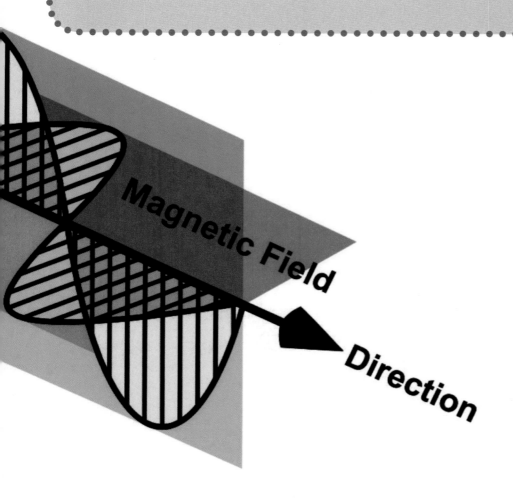

Magnetic Field

Direction

HOW DO CELL PHONE CALLS TRAVEL?

There's a small microphone within your cell phone. As you talk, your cell phone converts the up-and-down modulating pattern of your voice into electrical pulses. A special microchip within your cell phone takes these pulses and transforms them into numbers.

These strings of numbers are then gathered into an electromagnetic signal that is emitted from the antenna or aerial on the cell phone. Your conversation in the form of numbers speeds through the air at light speed until it gets to the closest cell phone tower.

The tower gets the pulses and then sends them to the base station. This station coordinates all calls within the local region of the network, which is described as a cell. From this station, the calls are sent to their destinations.

If a call is made from one cell phone to another within the same network, then it is routed to the station that is closest to the destination cell phone and then eventually to the cell phone you're calling.

Calls that started from one cell phone traveling to a cell phone on a different network or to a phone connected to a landline travel a lengthier pathway.

Sometimes they must travel a route that connects them to a main network before they can land at their final destination.

WHAT DO CELL PHONE TOWERS DO?

It might seem that cell phones aren't any different than walkie-talkies are. With a walkie-talkie, each one contains a sender as well as a receiver. When two people talk, their messages get bounced back and forth almost as if they are two ping pong players sending a ball back and forth over the net.

COMMUNICATION TOWER

CELLULAR COMMUNICATIONS TOWER

However, there are some issues with radio signals sent in this way. You can only use so many of them before calls from other walkie-talkies start interfering. In order to avoid this problem, cell phones were built to use much more sophisticated technology.

Cell phones can't beam signals very far. This isn't a failure in their design. In fact, they were created this way purposely.

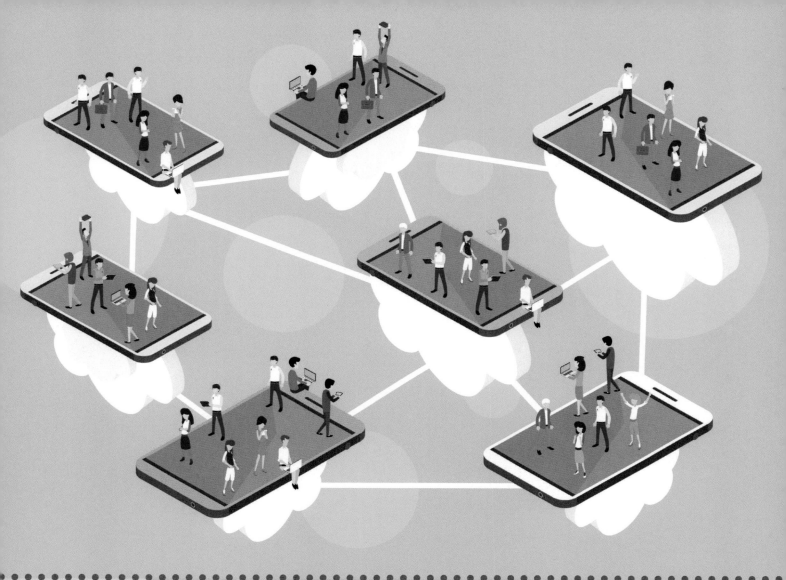

The goal is for the cell phone to transmit its signal to the closest tower, which is essentially a very high-powered antenna, and then on to the station.

TELECOMMUNICATION TOWERS

The job of the base station is to discern weak signals from lots of different cell phones and then route these signals so they get to their final destinations. The towers are enormous and are often mounted in places of high elevation, such as hills or tall buildings.

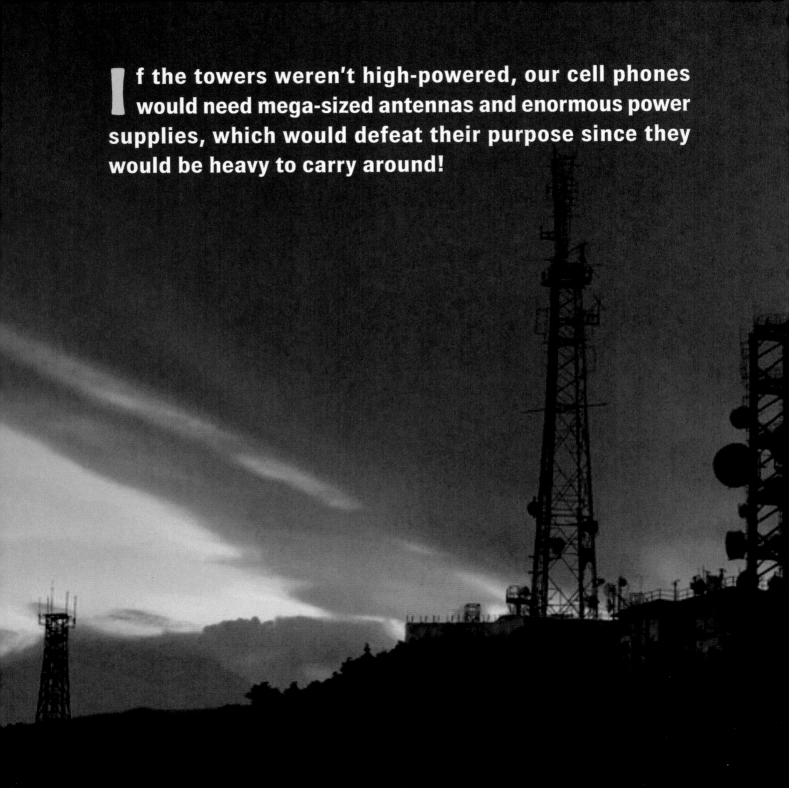

If the towers weren't high-powered, our cell phones would need mega-sized antennas and enormous power supplies, which would defeat their purpose since they would be heavy to carry around!

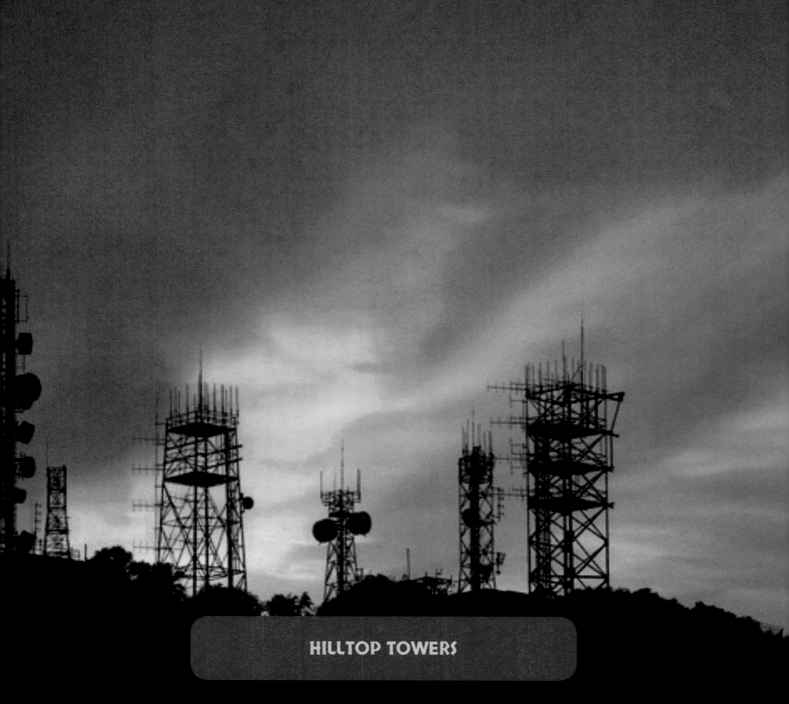

HILLTOP TOWERS

Your cell phone's signal is communicated to the closest cell, the one that has the most powerful signal.

It achieves this with the smallest amount of power possible. In this way, it retains its battery power as long as it can. This method also reduces the possibility that it will cause interference for nearby cell phones.

WHAT DO THE LOCAL CELLS DO?

Cells can be described as hexagons on a huge hexagonal grid. The phone carriers chop up an urban area into smaller areas that are about 3 miles by 3 miles. So, imagine a regular invisible hexagon inside that square and that's how a cell can be visualized. Each cell contains a main base station that is composed of a tower and a building that holds the radio equipment.

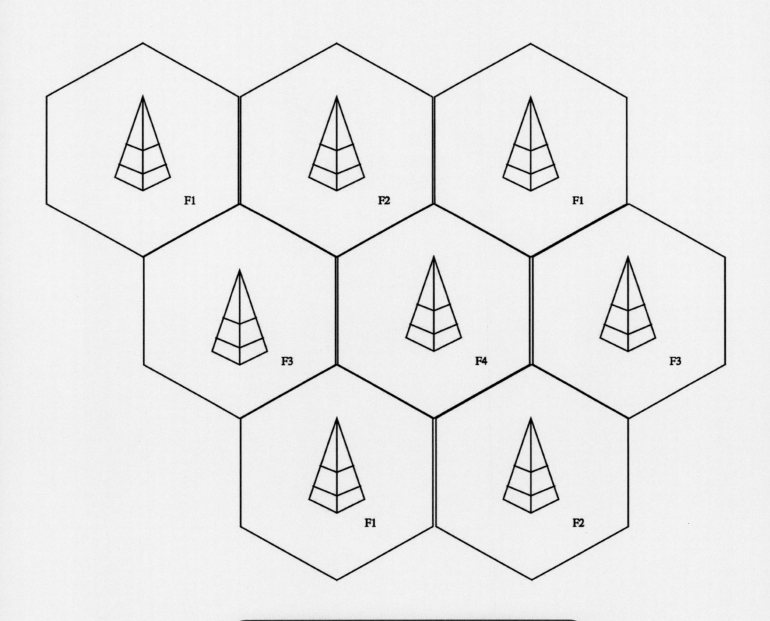

HEXAGONAL CELLS

There's a reason these cells need to be used and why cell phones don't communicate directly with each other. Suppose a bunch of people in your location wanted to send and receive calls using the same frequency of radio signals. With all these signals being sent in all different directions, the chances of calls interfering with each other and scrambling each other would be pretty high.

One way to possibly solve this would be for different calls to use different radio frequencies so they wouldn't interfere with each other. It would work as if there were a different radio station available for each call.

That might work if a small number of people were using their cell phones, but if there were thousands or millions of people using their phones at the same time there would be a need for the same number of radio frequencies, which wouldn't be practical.

The cells provide an elegant and practical solution to this problem. Depending on the amount of population, phone companies divide areas into cells. If the area is highly populated, the cell size is smaller.

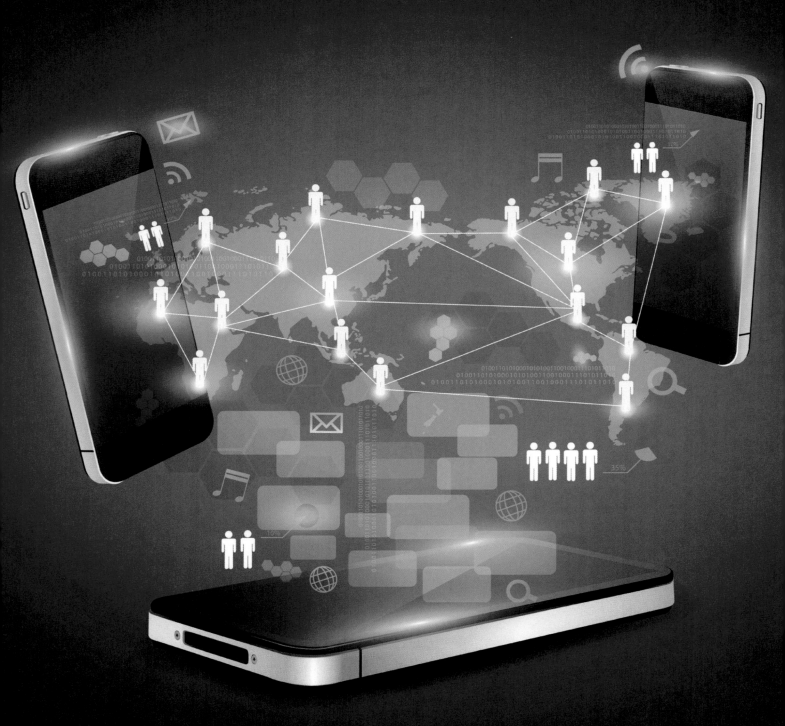

In rural areas, where not as many calls need to be handled, the cell size is larger. Because each cell uses the same set of frequencies as the cells that are its neighbors, it enables many more calls to be handled and routed at the same time. The larger the number of cells, the more calls can be routed efficiently.

WHAT'S THE DIFFERENCE BETWEEN CELL PHONES AND SMART PHONES?

Most cell phones today are actually smart phones. During the 1990s, cell phones had a lot less functions than they do today. At the beginning, they were mostly used for making phone calls without the inconvenience of wires. Gradually, more and more features were added until the cell phone evolved into a smart phone.

OLD CELLPHONE VS SMARTPHONE

Today's smart phones are similar to having a computer in your pocket. They have all the functionality of a telephone, but they also work as digital cameras. They have lots of other functions too.

They can play MP3 files like an iPod does, send text messages back and forth, and perform the same tasks as a laptop or tablet using a wide variety of software applications.

They also have a global positioning system, which can pinpoint your location and provide you with detailed maps on how to get places. All this functionality has been made possible because today's networks can carry the needed data.

GPS NAVIGATION SYSTEM IN CAR

SUMMARY

Unlike telephones that are connected to landlines, cell phones don't need any wires to work. As you talk on your cell phone, the up-and-down pattern of your voice is transformed into electrical signals. A small microchip inside your cell phone changes these electrical signals into a series of numbers. The numbers are broadcast via radio waves, which are electromagnetic energy. Instead of going from cell phone to cell phone, these signals go to local towers and base stations before they are routed to their destination.

Now that you've read about how cell phones work, you may want to read about the evolution of cell phones in the Baby Professor book From Cell Phones to VOIP: The Evolution of Communication Technology.

Visit

BABY PROFESSOR
EDUCATION KIDS

www.BabyProfessorBooks.com

to download Free Baby Professor eBooks
and view our catalog of new and exciting
Children's Books

Made in the USA
Monee, IL
15 January 2020